Celebration Times

Feasts and Seasons of the Church Year

Reproducible Handouts for Primary Grades

Active Learning for Catholic Kids

Hi-Time✳Pflaum

Dayton, OH

Celebration Times
Feasts and Seasons of the Church Year
Reproducible Handouts for Primary Grades
Active Learning for Catholic Kids

Cover design by Larissa Qvick
Interior design by Patricia Lynch

ISBN: 0-937997-49-8

Contents

Advent

Advent Saints ....Who Am I?

Advent Calendar .... My Advent Plans (2 pages)

Immaculate Conception: December 8 ....A Prayer to Mary

Our Lady of Guadalupe: December 12 .... The Beautiful Maiden

Christmas Time

Christmas .... On the Road to Bethlehem

The Baptism of the Lord ....I Join God's Family

Lent/Spring

Spring Holy and Feast Days .... Special Days of Spring

Signs and Symbols ....The Sign of the Day

Ash Wednesday .... My Lenten Resolution Egg (2 pages)

St. Patrick's Day: March 17..Three in One

St. Joseph's Day: March 19 .... The Journeys of Joseph (2 pages)

Holy Week .... Who's Who in Holy Week

Triduum ....The Great Days of Holy Week

Easter Time

Easter...A Basket of Good Wishes (2 pages)

Pentecost .... The Holy Spirit Helps You Choose

Ordinary Time

St. Francis of Assisi: October 4 ....He Talked to the Animals

All Saints Day: November 1 .... Which Saint?

Thanksgiving ....Give Thanks: A Prayer Service

At Any Time

The Liturgical Seasons .... Church Cycle Circle (2 pages)

Feasts of Mary ....Mary, Our Mother

Who Am I?

Name _____

Can you guess who these Advent saints are? Put the number for the correct answer in the box provided.

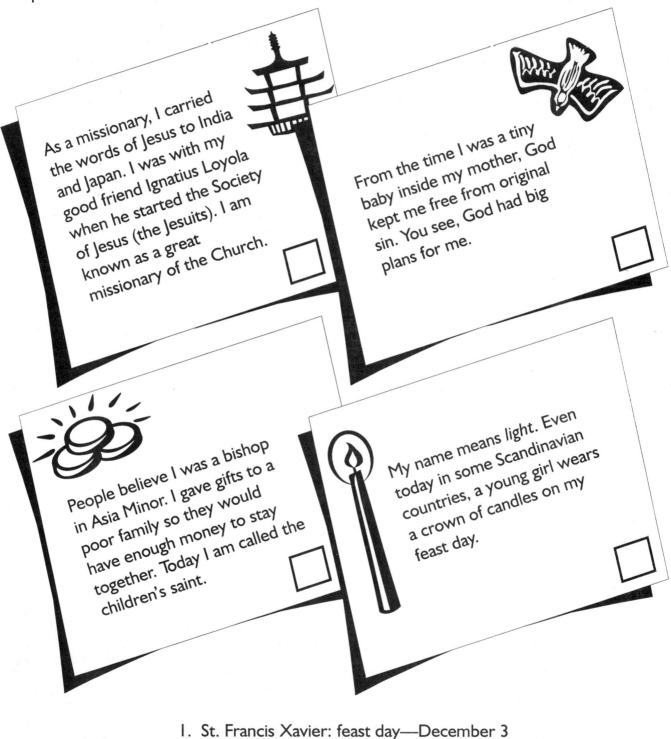

As a missionary, I carried the words of Jesus to India and Japan. I was with my good friend Ignatius Loyola when he started the Society of Jesus (the Jesuits). I am known as a great missionary of the Church.

From the time I was a tiny baby inside my mother, God kept me free from original sin. You see, God had big plans for me.

People believe I was a bishop in Asia Minor. I gave gifts to a poor family so they would have enough money to stay together. Today I am called the children's saint.

My name means *light*. Even today in some Scandinavian countries, a young girl wears a crown of candles on my feast day.

1. St. Francis Xavier: feast day—December 3
2. St. Nicholas: feast day—December 6
3. Immaculate Conception: feast day—December 8
4. St. Lucy: feast day—December 13

My Advent Plans

Name _____

Complete your Advent calendar. It will be your own reminder of how you can use your Advent time best.

1. First, find out what day of the week Christmas falls on this year. Then put 25 on that day of the last week of your calendar.

2. Now find the Sunday before Christmas. Write "4th Sunday of Advent" in that space. Then find the 3rd, 2nd, and 1st Sundays of Advent and write their names in the right spaces.

3. Start numbering backwards from Christmas Day. Put the date numbers in the upper right-hand corner of each space.

4. The 1st Sunday of Advent may occur in November. When you number, remember that November has 30 days. So the day before December 1 is November 30. Some squares on your completed calendar will be left empty.

5. Now add the major saints' days and feast days of Advent. Write their names in the correct spaces.

   December 3: St. Francis Xavier
   December 6: St. Nicholas
   December 8: Immaculate Conception
      (Holy Day)
   December 9: Blessed Juan Diego
   December 12: Our Lady of Guadalupe
   December 13: St. Lucy

6. Color the 1st, 2nd, and 4th Sundays of Advent violet or purple. Color the 3rd Sunday rose or pink. The priest wears rose on the 3rd Sunday because we're happy that Christmas is not too far away.

7. Now write in the blank spaces some of the things you can do during Advent that will help others or will put them in a better mood for Christmas. Here are some suggestions, but be sure to write some of your own.

   - Plan presents to make
   - Be nice to little kids
   - Do homework with a smile
   - Help decorate
   - Help with cleaning
   - Say hello to a new kid in school
   - Smile at my family
   - Make up a prayer of my own for Advent
   - Find out about Advent saints

   - _____
   - _____
   - _____
   - _____
   - _____

8. Decorate your calendar with symbols of Christmas. Then put it in your room at home or on the refrigerator.

My Advent Plans

Advent Calendar: Year _____

Completed by _____

Sunday	Monday	Tuesday	Wednesday	Thursday	Friday	Saturday

A Prayer to Mary

Name _____

On December 8 we honor Mary because she lived her entire life and never did anything wrong. She never sinned. "Immaculate Conception" means that from the moment Mary began life as a tiny baby inside her mother's body, God kept Mary from all sin.

You probably know the prayer called the "Hail Mary." Can you also make up your own prayer to honor Mary? Use the Word List and fill in the blanks with a word or phrase that will finish this prayer.

Hail Mary...Because you are the Mother of Jesus and the Mother of the Church,

you are my _____ too. I think you are _____

because you _____. God blessed you a lot while you lived on

_____. But you had _____ times too. One was

when _____ died on the _____. Be with me

during my _____ times and my _____ times

too. I love you. Amen.

Word List

Jesus	never sinned	cross
wonderful	Mother	earth
good	sad	bad

The Beautiful Maiden

Name _____

December 12 is the feast of Our Lady of Guadalupe, whose story is told here in words and shown in pictures. Draw a line from each block of words to its correct picture. If you'd like, cut out the picture and the words. Then, on another sheet of paper, arrange the pictures in the correct order and paste the right words under each picture.

On his way to Mass near Mexico City in 1531, Juan Diego saw a Native American maiden dressed in Aztec clothes.

The maiden told Juan Diego to ask the bishop of Mexico to build a chapel where she appeared. But the bishop refused.

The maiden told Juan Diego to gather roses to prove to the bishop who she was. Juan put them in his cloak.

When Juan Diego opened his cloak for the bishop, they both saw a miracle. A picture of the Lady had appeared on the cloak. It was December 12, 1531.

On the Road to Bethlehem

Name _____

Mary and Joseph need to go from Nazareth to Bethlehem, but there are many dangers along the way. Can you help them find a safe path? When you finish showing them the way, fill in the correct letters to answer the question below.

CLIFF
1 4

NAZARETH

BAD STORM
8   5   7

THIEVES
6 2

ROCKS
3   9

BETHLEHEM

When Mary and Joseph got to Bethlehem, Jesus was born. What do we call that day?

___ ___ ___ ___ ___ ___ ___ ___ ___
 1   2   3   4   5   6   7   8   9

I Join God's Family

Name _____

Jesus didn't have to be baptized to become a member of God's family. After all, Jesus is God—the leader of the family. Jesus was baptized to show us what to do. He wanted us to know how important it is to answer the call to be baptized.

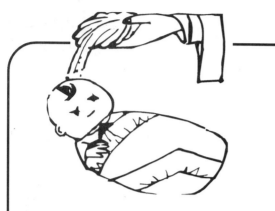

Try to learn as much as you can about your own baptism, then fill in the blanks. Ask someone to help you if you need to.

1. The name I was given at baptism:

_____.

2. The names of my godparents:

_____

and _____.

3. The church where I was baptized:

_____.

4. The city and state or province the church is in:

_____.

5. The date of my baptism:

_____.

6. My age at baptism: _____.

7. What I wore

8. How I behaved

_____.

9. How my family and friends spent the rest of the day:

_____

_____.

10. On the day I was baptized, I became part of another family—the huge family of Jesus' followers. Here are the names of some of the people who are now my brothers and sisters in Christ because they have also been baptized into Jesus' family.

_____

_____

_____

_____

_____

Special Days
of Spring

Name _____

From the following list, choose the correct day that is described below.

1. Ascension Thursday
2. Ash Wednesday
3. Easter Sunday
4. Pentecost Sunday
5. Good Friday
6. Passion/Palm Sunday

- Lent begins on this day.

  _____

- On this day we remember how the people celebrated when Jesus came to Jerusalem.

  _____

- We remember Jesus' death on the cross on this day.

  _____

- This is the day we celebrate Jesus' victory over death.

  _____

- Jesus returns to the Father on this day.

  _____

- On this day Jesus and the Father send the Holy Spirit to be with Jesus' followers and his Church forever.

  _____

Make up your own prayer to say with your family on one of the spring Holy Days or Feast Days. Write it here.

The Sign of the Day

Name _____

Certain signs remind us of certain important days. For example, a cake with candles reminds us of a birthday. Evergreens with bows of red ribbon remind us of Christmas.

Write the name of the sign beside its picture. Then write on the line the Holy Day or Feast Day that each sign reminds you of: Ash Wednesday, Passion/Palm Sunday, Good Friday, Easter, Ascension, or Pentecost.

Now find the secret message by writing the correct letter above each of these numbers.

‾‾ ‾‾ ‾‾ ‾‾ ‾‾ ‾‾
1 2 3 4 5 6

‾‾ ‾‾ ‾‾   ‾‾ ‾‾ ‾‾ ‾‾
7 8 9   10 11 12 13

My Lenten Resolution Egg

Name _____

Ash Wednesday is the first day of Lent. During Lent, we try to do something to make ourselves better and our world a better place. We call a promise to try to do better a *resolution*.

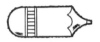

Decide on one thing you will do this Lent to improve yourself or your world. This is your resolution. Write it on the egg, then color the egg light purple. (Purple is the color for Lent.)

Cut out your egg and paste it onto a heavy piece of colored paper. Cut around the edge of the egg so that you have a sturdy "Lenten egg." Hang it at home where you can see it every day.

Every Sunday during Lent, think back on your week and decide how well you did with your resolution. Check the box that best describes your efforts.

Bring your egg to your last class before Easter. Look at your results. Then trace around your egg on a pretty piece of paper and cut out a new "Easter" egg. Paste this one over your Lenten egg. Decorate your Easter egg any way you like. Poke a hole near the top of your egg and pull a ribbon through it to serve as a hanger. Display your egg on your class bulletin board or at home to remind you how you tried to improve yourself or the world and prepare for Easter.

My Lenten Resolution Egg

Name _____

My Resolution

_____

_____

1st Sunday of Lent	☐ I did great. ☐ I did okay. ☐ I'll do better next week.	
2nd Sunday of Lent	☐ I did great. ☐ I did okay. ☐ I'll do better next week.	
3rd Sunday of Lent	☐ I did great. ☐ I did okay. ☐ I'll do better next week.	
4th Sunday of Lent	☐ I did great. ☐ I did okay. ☐ I'll do better next week.	
5th Sunday of Lent	☐ I did great. ☐ I did okay. ☐ I'll do better next week.	
Palm/Passion Sunday	☐ I did great. ☐ I did okay. ☐ I'll do better next week.	

Three in One

Name _____

Connect the dots. You will see the plant St. Patrick used to teach the Irish people about the Trinity. After you have completed the picture, color it green.

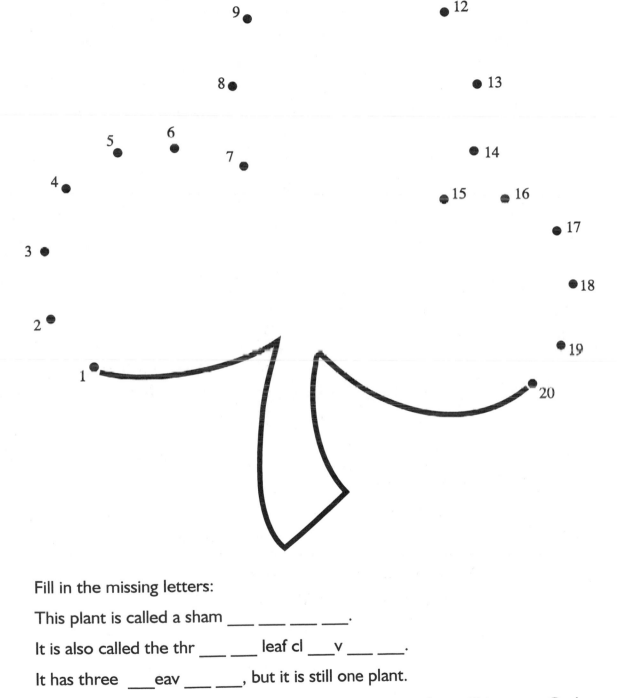

Fill in the missing letters:

This plant is called a sham ___ ___ ___ ___.

It is also called the thr ___ ___ leaf cl ___ v ___ ___.

It has three ___eav ___ ___, but it is still one plant.

The Trinity means that there are three pers ___ ___s, but still just one God.

The Journeys of Joseph

Name _____

Feast Day—March 19

Place the correct Journey number in the circles along the paths that Joseph traveled. Color the pathways as directed.

Journey 1 St. Joseph and Mary travel from their hometown of Nazareth to Bethlehem, where Jesus is born. Use a red crayon or marker to trace their path from Nazareth to Bethlehem.

Journey 3 St. Joseph has a dream telling him that King Herod is dead and it is safe to go home. Use a blue crayon or marker to trace the Holy Family's path from Egypt back to Nazareth.

★

Journey 4 When Jesus is twelve years old, the Holy Family travels to Jerusalem for Passover. Use an orange crayon or marker to trace the path from Nazareth to Jerusalem.

★

Journey 5 After finding Jesus talking with the teachers in the temple at Jerusalem, Joseph, Mary, and Jesus make the journey once again to their home in Nazareth, where Jesus grows up. Use a yellow crayon or marker to trace the path from Jerusalem to Nazareth.

★

Journey 2 After Jesus is born, Joseph takes Jesus and Mary to Egypt to avoid King Herod's anger. Use a green crayon or marker to trace their path from Bethlehem to Egypt.

Nazareth is where St. Joseph dies. Because he dies with Mary and Jesus at his side, he is the patron of a happy death. Use a purple crayon or marker to circle the town of Nazareth.

Name _____

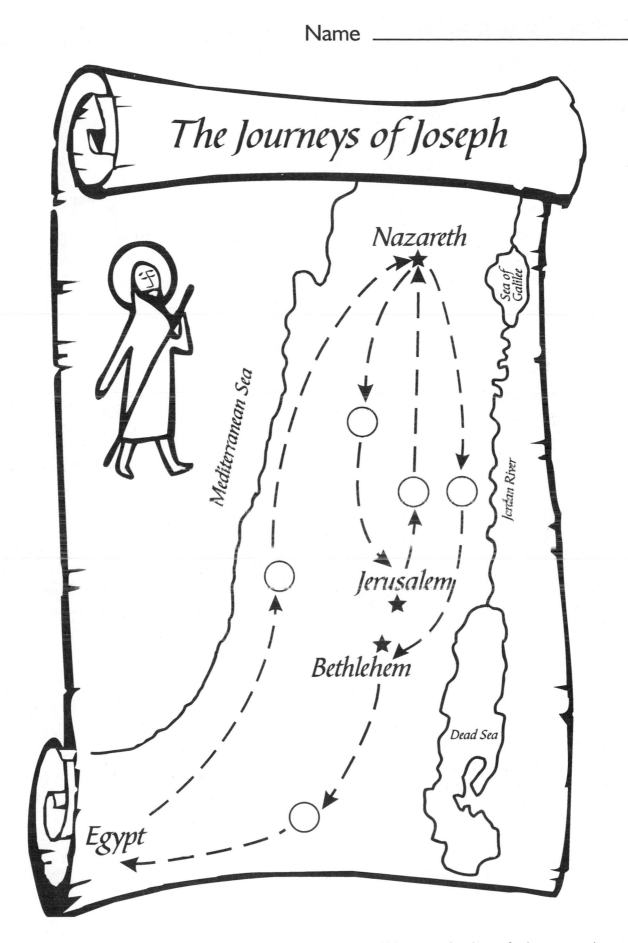

The Journeys of Joseph

Nazareth

Sea of Galilee

Mediterranean Sea

Jordan River

Jerusalem

Bethlehem

Dead Sea

Egypt

Who's Who in Holy Week

If you don't know the answer to the question, look in one of the Bible verses to find it.

A. Who handed Jesus over to his enemies for a payment of 30 pieces of silver? (Matthew 26:14; Mark 14:10; Luke 22:3; John 13:2)

_____

B. What did Jesus bless first at the Last Supper? (Matthew 26:26; Mark 14:22)

_____

C. What was the name of the garden where Jesus prayed? (Matthew 26:36; Mark 14:32)

_____

D. Who denied Jesus three times? (Matthew 26:75; Mark 14:72; Luke 22:61)

_____

E. Who handed Jesus over to be crucified? (Matthew 27:24; Mark 15:15; Luke 23:24; John 19:6)

_____

F. What was the name of the man who buried Jesus? (Matthew 27:57; Mark 15:43; Luke 23:50; John 19:38)

_____

Now arrange your answers to finish the crossword puzzle.

ACROSS
2. Answer to F
4. Answer to D
5. Answer to A
6. Answer to E

DOWN
1. Answer to C
3. Answer to B

The Great Days of Holy Week

Name _____

Make this reminder about the Great Days of Holy Week to put on your refrigerator at home.

Decide which day is described by reading the clues inside each circle. Here are the days to choose from: Holy Thursday, Good Friday, Holy Saturday, Easter Sunday. Write the correct day on the line at the top of the circle.

Cut each circle on the dotted line, and cut a hole at the top of each circle. String the circles together in the right order. Hang them on your refrigerator.

Today is

_____

We kneel before the cross
and honor it.
The cross reminds us how
Jesus suffered
and died for us.

Today is

_____

Today is the day Jesus rose
from the dead.
We celebrate and have fun
with our families and
friends.

Today is

_____

We remember the supper
Jesus shared with his friends.

Today is

_____

The priest lights the Easter
candle and blesses water.
Often, people are baptized.

A Basket of Good Wishes

Name _____

Make an Easter basket to give to a parent, grandparent, or friend. This basket will carry your good wishes to a special person this Easter.

1. Color the basket.

2. Cut around the basket on the dotted lines.

3. Cut along the dotted line on the inside of the basket. Be careful not to cut through the handles of the basket.

4. Paste or tape an 8½" x 11" piece of paper behind the basket. Use paste or tape only on the outside edges so that your basket has an open pocket. This will let you put your eggs in the basket.

HAPPY EASTER!
TO:
FROM:

Name _____

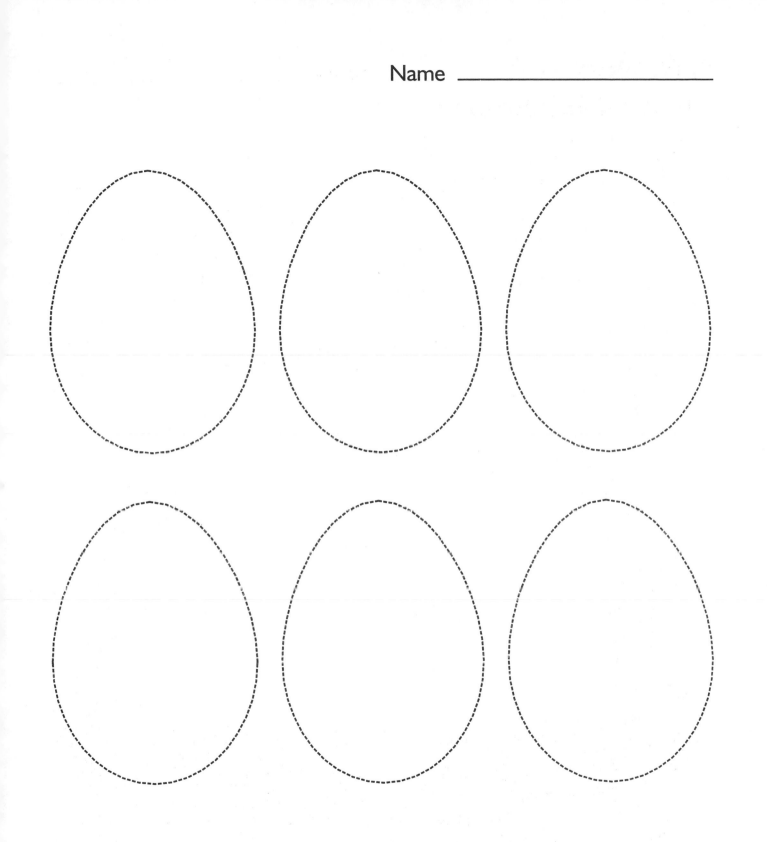

On each of the eggs, write a special message to the person who will get the egg. You might want to tell the person why you like him or her so much. You might also tell about some good things you plan to do for that person. Color or decorate the eggs, cut them out, and put them in the basket you have already made. Your Easter basket is ready to deliver!

The Holy Spirit Helps You Choose

Name _____

On Pentecost Sunday we remember that Jesus and the Father sent the Holy Spirit to all of Jesus' followers. The Spirit comes to us today in the sacraments of baptism and confirmation. The Spirit helps us choose to do the right thing at the right time.

Look at each story below. What would the Holy Spirit want you to do or say in each case? Write your answer on the lines provided.

1. Two of your friends have taken a little kid's hat and are tossing it back and forth to keep it away from her. What will you say to your friends?

_____

_____

2. A classmate who doesn't have very many toys or nice clothes just got a new bike. He talks a lot about how great his bike is. You know your bike is much better than his. What will you say?

_____

_____

3. Your little sister has been asking you all day to play with her, and you've ignored her. She gets into your room and accidentally upsets a jigsaw puzzle you and your dad had worked on for a week. What will you do?

_____

_____

4. Your mother had a bad day at work. Then the soup she was making for supper boiled over and made a mess. She just asked if you would turn off the TV, feed the dog, and take him for a walk. What do you answer?

_____

_____

He Talked to the Animals

Name _____

Directions: Draw a line between the two parts of each sentence about St. Francis of Assisi. The first one has been done for you.

He was baptized Giovanni (joh-VAHN-ee), which is Italian for John,

Because Francis' father was rich

One day Francis saw a poor leper, but

Francis loved God's creatures so much that

Francis started a religious order that

Francis always wanted

Shortly before he died, Francis

Francis died

Francis said,

to be as much like Jesus as possible.

Francis was able to live the life of a big spender when he was young.

practiced poverty and served those in need.

but his father liked France so much that he called his son Francis.

"It's not right for a servant of God to show a sad or gloomy face."

Instead of turning away, Francis gave the man money and kissed his hand.

he preached to the birds and rescued lambs that were going to be killed.

received the *stigmata*, the wounds of Christ, which bled from time to time.

in 1226 and was named a saint two years later.

Which Saint?

Name _____

Read these short stories about five saints. Then answer the questions below.

St. Anthony of Padua (1195-1231) Anthony preached so well that he led many people to find Jesus. Even today people ask St. Anthony to help them find something they have lost.

 **St. Bernadette** (1844-1879) Mary, the mother of Jesus, used Bernadette to bring millions of people closer to Jesus. Mary appeared to 14-year-old Bernadette at Lourdes, France. Mary asked Bernadette to uncover a spring of water that would cure sick people. Since then, hundreds of thousands of people have come to Lourdes, and many have been cured.

 **St. Vincent de Paul** (1580-1660) Vincent cared about helping the poor and the sick. Today many Catholic parishes have a St. Vincent de Paul Society to help the poor and suffering.

St. Ann is said to be the mother of Mary, who is the mother of Jesus. Jesus said all of us are his sisters and brothers. What relation does this make St. Ann to all of us?

1. A new homeless shelter is being built in your city and you are asked to name it after a saint. Which saint would you choose?

   _____

   Why? _____

   _____

2. You've been arguing with your family all day. You want to talk to your grandmother and ask her how to make peace with everyone, but she lives a thousand miles away. What saint could you ask for help?

   _____

   Why? _____

   _____

3. Your cousin is sick and you want to pray for the nurses and doctors who are caring for him. Which saint would you pray to?

   _____

   Why? _____

   _____

4. You got lost in the woods during a family outing. Which saint could you ask for help to find your way?

   _____

   Why? _____

   _____

Give Thanks: A Prayer Service

Name _____

Draw pictures of things you are especially thankful for: a person or persons and something in nature. When you finish, cut out the squares and use them in this Thanksgiving Prayer Service.

To Leader: Set a candle and a large basket on a small table. Light the candle as everyone sings an appropriate song. Extinguish the candle while all are singing the closing song.

A Person or Persons

Something in Nature

Leader: We gather to offer God our thanks for the many good things we have received in the past year. Sing praise to the Lord.

All: *Give thanks to God's holy name.*

Leader: Let us begin by thinking of a special person or persons for whom we are grateful. As I call your name, bring your drawing forward and put it in the basket. If you wish, you may tell us the name of the person.

Leader: For all of these people, God, we are grateful to you. Sing praise to the Lord.

All: *Give thanks to God's holy name.*

(The Leader then moves on to something in nature for which students are thankful, following the same procedure as above.)

Leader: O, God, we ask you to accept our thanks that we offer you today. We know all good things come from you and we humbly say: Sing praise to the Lord.

All: *Give thanks to God's holy name.*

Church Cycle Circle

Name _____

The Church year is divided into seasons. Do you know the names of the Church seasons? They are Advent, Christmas, Ordinary Time, Lent, Easter, and then more Ordinary Time. Every year these seasons repeat themselves too, just like the seasons of nature. We call this the Church cycle.

The Church uses special colors for each season to remind us what that season is about. Learning the Church seasons, their colors, and what the colors mean can be fun. Just follow these directions and soon you will have a Church Cycle Circle that will help you remember all the seasons of the Church year.

1. Color the Lent and Advent strips purple. Purple is the color that reminds us to get ready for something—to prepare ourselves. In Advent we get ready to celebrate the birth of Jesus at Christmas. In Lent, we get ready to celebrate Jesus' death and resurrection. The priest wears purple during these seasons.

2. Easter Time and Christmas Time are the happiest times of the year. Color them white or leave them white. White shows joy. The priest wears white at these happy times of year.

3. Green is the color of growth and hope. During Ordinary Time we grow in faith, and the priest wears green during Mass. Color Ordinary Time green.

4. Now cut out each of the paper strips on the dotted lines.

5. Look first for Advent. The 1st Sunday of Advent is the beginning of the Church year. Now find Christmas Time. Tape Advent and Christmas Time together to make one strip. Remember that Advent comes before Christmas.

6. Now find the short Ordinary Time and tape it next to Christmas.

7. Find Lent and tape it next in line. Do you remember what we're getting ready for in Lent? That's right. The answer is Jesus' death and resurrection. Tape Easter Time right after Lent.

8. The longest and last season of the Church year is Ordinary Time again. Tape it right after Easter Time. Then, to complete the year, tape the end of Ordinary Time to the beginning of Advent. Now your Church Cycle Circle is done! Take it home and put it where you can see it often. It will help you remember the seasons of the Church year and what they mean.

Name _____

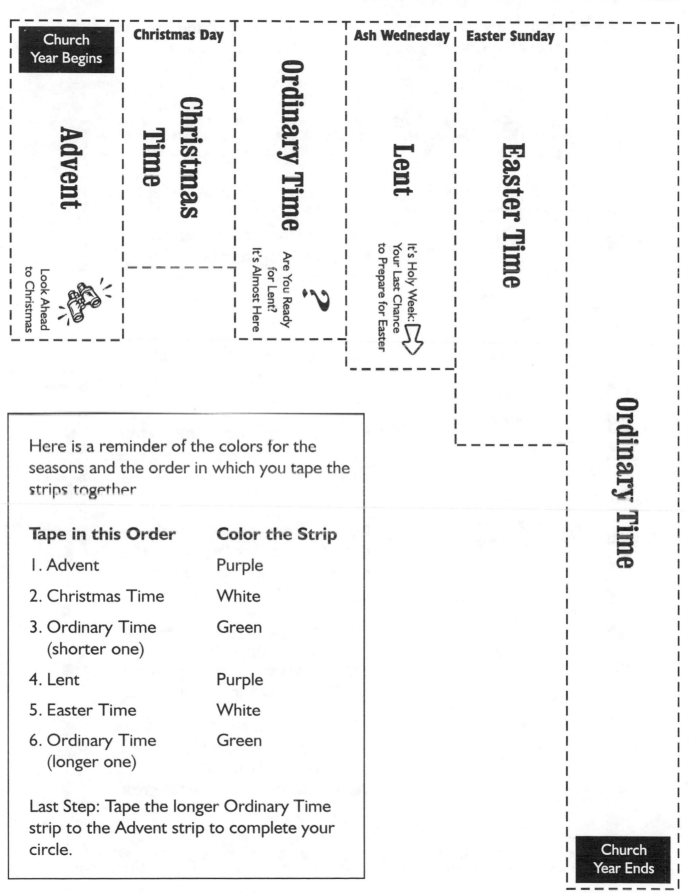

Church Year Begins

Christmas Day

Ash Wednesday | Easter Sunday

Advent

Look Ahead to Christmas

Christmas Time

Ordinary Time

Are You Ready for Lent? It's Almost Here

Lent

It's Holy Week: Your Last Chance to Prepare for Easter

Easter Time

Ordinary Time

Church Year Ends

Here is a reminder of the colors for the seasons and the order in which you tape the strips together

Tape in this Order	Color the Strip
1. Advent	Purple
2. Christmas Time	White
3. Ordinary Time (shorter one)	Green
4. Lent	Purple
5. Easter Time	White
6. Ordinary Time (longer one)	Green

Last Step: Tape the longer Ordinary Time strip to the Advent strip to complete your circle.

Mary, Our Mother

Name _____

Here are six Feasts of Mary that are celebrated throughout the Church year. Try to decide what each feast asks us to remember. Draw a line from the square under the feast to the circle in front of each remembrance. The first one has been done for you.

Feast Day

Mary, Mother of God
January 1
□

Annunciation
March 25
□

Visitation
May 31
□

Assumption
August 15
□

Immaculate Conception
December 8
□

Our Lady of Guadalupe
December 12
□

Meaning

○ On this day we remember that Mary visited her cousin Elizabeth, the mother of John the Baptist. Elizabeth recognized how important Mary was in God's plan. We use Elizabeth's words often in prayer. See Luke 1:42.

○ On this day we honor Mary under a title the Church gave her in its earliest years.

○ As an honor to Native American peoples, Mary appeared to Juan Diego as an Aztec maiden outside Mexico City in 1531.

○ Mary is patron of the U.S. under this title. We honor her for being without sin. She used this title when she appeared to St. Bernadette in 1858.

○ When an angel speaks, people listen. Mary listened to the Archangel Gabriel and said yes to God's plan for her. Read about it in Luke 1:26-38.

○ Like all human beings, Mary died. But she was greatly honored by being taken bodily to heaven after her death. Today we celebrate this great event.

Notes to Teacher

Who Am I?

St. Francis Xavier was the missionary to India and Japan.

St. Nicholas was the bishop in Asia Minor.

The Immaculate Conception is the baby born free of original sin.

St. Lucy's name means *light*.

On the Road to Bethlehem

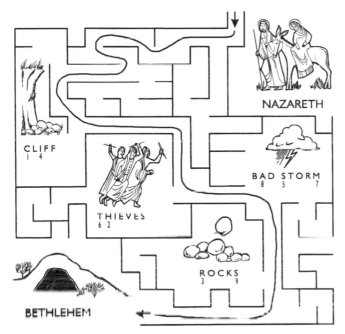

Word Answer: Christmas

Special Days of Spring

Lent begins on *Ash Wednesday*.

Jesus entered Jerusalem on *Palm/Passion Sunday*.

We commemorate Jesus' death on *Good Friday*.

We celebrate Jesus' victory over death on *Easter Sunday*.

Jesus returns to the Father on *Ascension Thursday*.

Jesus and the Father sent the Holy Spirit on *Pentecost Sunday*.

The Sign of the Day

Signs: ashes; fire; cloud; palm; cross; butterfly

Secret Message: Praise the Lord.

Three in One

shamrock; three leaf clover; leaves; persons

Who's Who in Holy Week

A. Judas
B. bread
C. Gethsemane
D. Peter
E. Pilate
F. Joseph

He Talked to the Animals

1. (Done)
2. ...Francis was able to live the life of a big spender when he was young.
3. ...instead of turning away, Francis gave the man money and kissed his hand.
4. ...he preached to the birds and rescued lambs that were going to be killed.
5. ...practiced poverty and served those in need.
6. ...to be as much like Jesus as possible.
7. ...received the stigmata, the wounds of Christ, which bled from time to time.
8. ...in 1226 and was named a saint two years later.
9. ..."It's not right for a servant of God to show a sad or gloomy face."

Which Saint?

1. St. Vincent de Paul
2. St. Ann
3. St. Bernadette
4. St. Anthony

Mary, Our Mother

• Mary, Mother of God—a title the Church gave Mary in its earliest years.

• Annunciation—the Archangel Gabriel asked Mary to accept God's plan for her.

• Visitation—Mary visited Elizabeth.

• Assumption—Mary was taken into heaven after her death.

• Immaculate Conception—Mary was without sin and is patron of the U.S. under this title.

Active Learning for Catholic Kids

Celebration Times

Feasts and Seasons of the Church Year

What day do we celebrate with heart-shaped cards and candy?
On what day do we hunt for dyed eggs and marshmallow chickens?
Name the season of the year when we race our sleds down a snow-packed hill.

Do you think any primary-grader would have trouble answering these questions?
Probably not.

But how many could say what we await during the Advent season or why we make special sacrifices during Lent? How many would know what the feast of the Immaculate Conception means or when the Church year begins and ends?

Celebration Times: Feasts and Seasons of the Church Year is part of the Active Learning for Catholic Kids series — activity books designed and written to help children in the primary grades understand Church teaching. In *Celebration Times*, children learn about the Church's rich liturgical cycle, the reasons behind special feasts, and the meanings of traditional Church customs.

Active Learning for Catholic Kids

Filled with fun activities, games, and crafts, this series of easy-to-use books helps reinforce religion lessons, highlight parish life, and celebrate special feasts. Economical too! Each page is reproducible so you can make as many copies as you need.

Other Titles for Primary Level

*The Sacraments • Let's Pray • The Saints
Exploring My Catholic Church • Caring for God's Creation
A Journey with Jesus • Living by God's Rules*

Call 800-543-4383 for titles in the following series:
*Active Learning for Catholic Kids: Intermediate Grades
Active Learning for Catholic Teens: Junior High*

Celebration Times: Feasts and Seasons of the Church Year
Sample Contents

• Who Am I? (Advent Saints)
• The Great Days of Holy Week (Triduum)
• The Beautiful Maiden (Lady of Guadalupe)
• Church Cycle Circle (The Liturgical Seasons)
• I Join God's Family (Baptism of the Lord)
• Mary, Our Mother (Feasts of Mary)

0-937997-49-8 $7.95   Children/Religion/Liturgy

Hi-Time✳Pflaum
330 Progress Road • Dayton, OH 45449
Phone: 1-800-543-4383 • Fax: 1-800-370-4450
Service@HiTimePflaum.com • www.HiTimePflaum.com

3400

ISBN 0-937997-49-8
50795>
9 780937 997499